Sounds in the House

Sonidos en la casa

A Mystery

BANG!

CLACK!

CREEK!

By Karl Beckstrand
Illustrated by Channing Jones

D1262579

Sounds in the House

Spanish vowels have one sound each: *a = ah e = eh i = ee o = oh u = oo*.
Every vowel should be pronounced (except for the *u* after a *q* [*que* is pronounced *keh*]). In Spanish, the letter *j* is pronounced as an English *h* (and the letter *h* is silent), *ll* sounds like a *y* (or a j in some countries), and *ñ* has an *ny* sound (*año* sounds like *ah-nyo*).

Spanish nouns are masculine or feminine and are usually preceded by an article: *la* = feminine *the*; *el* = masculine *the*; *una* = feminine *a* or *one*; *un* = masculine *a* or *one*. Articles (and -s/-es after nouns) reflect plural: *las* = plural feminine *the*; *los* = plural masculine *the*; *unas* = feminine *some*; *unos* = masculine *some*. In Spanish, the accent is generally on the first or second syllable of simple words. Words with four or more syllables often have the accent on the third syllable. Variations occur with conjugation. If there's an accent mark—follow that!

Las combinaciones de letras en inglés pueden cambiar los sonidos por completo: *ck* se pronuncia como *k; wr* se pronuncia como *r; ee* se pronuncia *i; qu* se pronuncia *cu; ai* se pronuncia *ey; ll* se pronuncia *l;* y *gh* no tiene sonido en medio, y al final, de la mayoria de las palabras. El sonido de *ch* (de chico) se ocupa al comenzar palabras, en el medio, y al final también. Para pronunciar *sh*, manten la mandíbula cerrada y los labios abiertos; sopla aire entre los dientes (al añadir la vocal que le siga, si hay.) Para pronunciar *th*, pon la lengua entre los dientes de adelante (arriba y abajo) y sopla un poquito de aire sobre la lengua.

Los sustantivos en inglés no tienen género; se usa *the* para *la, el, las,* y *los*. Algunas palabras en inglés — a pesar de escribirse de forma diferente — terminan con el mismo sonido (se pronuncian como si se escribieran igual al final): *guy* y *pie, do* y *boo, throw* y *go, trees* y *breeze*.

Premio Publishing & Gozo Books, LLC
Midvale, UT, USA
ISBN: 978-0-6154423-0-3

Text Copyright © 2011 Karl Beckstrand
Illustrations Copyright © 2011 Channing Jones

Pida este libro en ingles o bilingüe / This book is available in English, bilingual, and e-book versions: Premiobooks.com. Descuentos para pedidos en volumen y para organizaciones educativas o caritativas. Discounts available for fundraising, bulk, school, and charitable donation orders.

Libros online GRATIS / FREE online books: Premiobooks.com

I hear a noise,
SOUNDS in the house!

¡Escucho un ruido,
SONIDOS en la casa!

A squeak from the door,
steps on the floor,
a creak on the stair,

IT'S RAISING MY HAIR!

Un chirrido desde la puerta, pasos en
el piso, un rechinar desde el escalón.
¡Los pelos se me levantan del temor!

El reloj hace tic tac.
Una polilla golpea contra
la ventana.

The clock ticks.
A moth taps my
window.

The water
heater goes,
TAT TAT TAT

El calentador
de agua dice:
TATO TATO

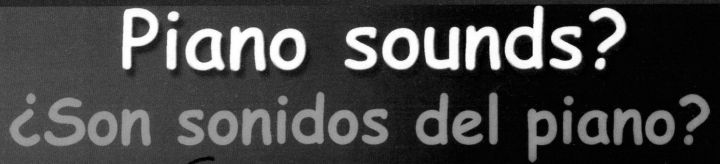

Las cañerías gimen. El refrigerador zzzzumba.

Pipes moan.
The refrigerator HUMMMMMS.

Trees creak in the breeze.

Los árboles rechinan en la brisa.

The furnace roars to life

El calefactor
brama con vida

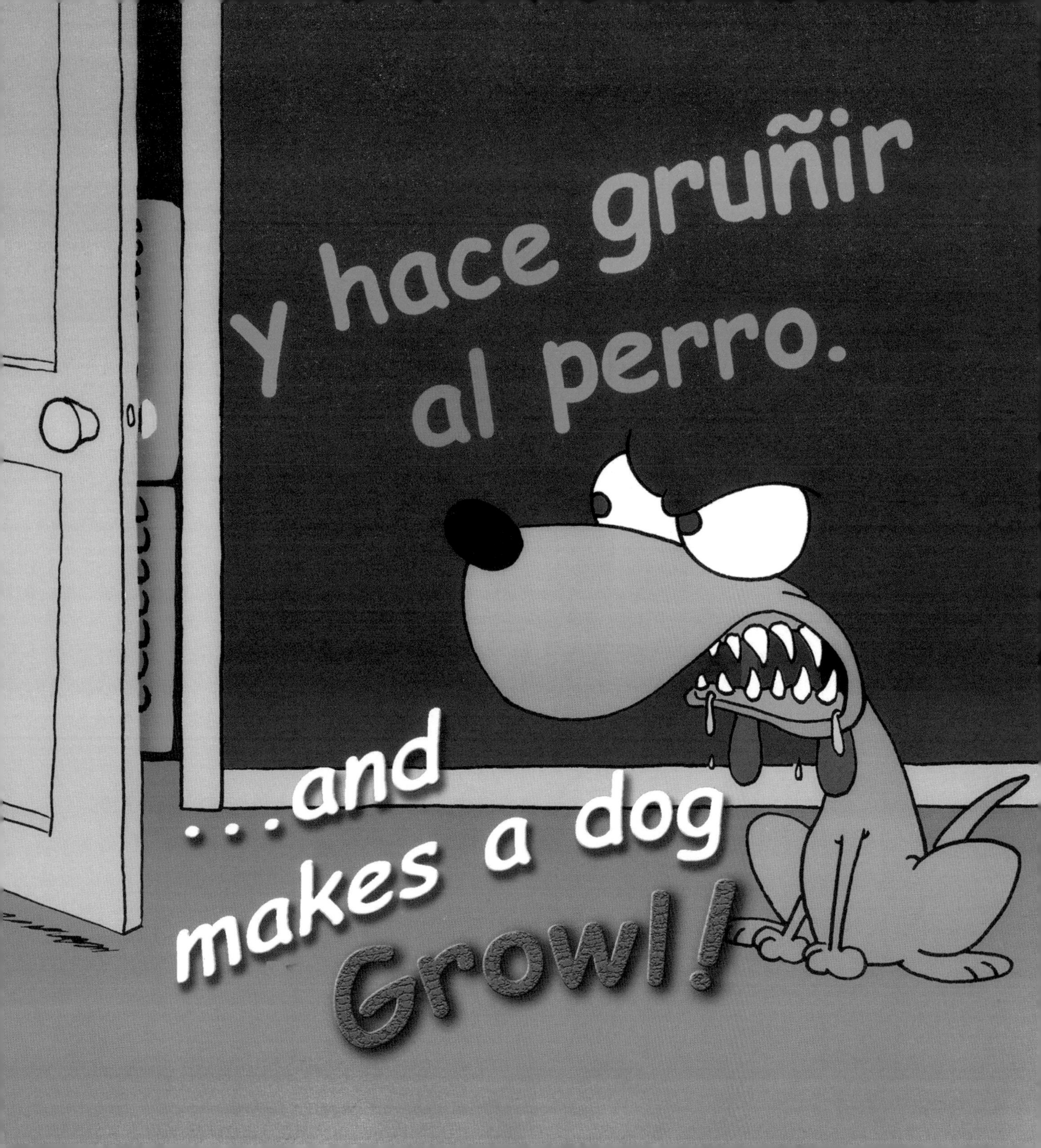
Y hace gruñir
al perro.
...and
makes a dog
Growl!

WUMP!

A DOOR SLAMS!

¡Una puerta se cierra de golpe!

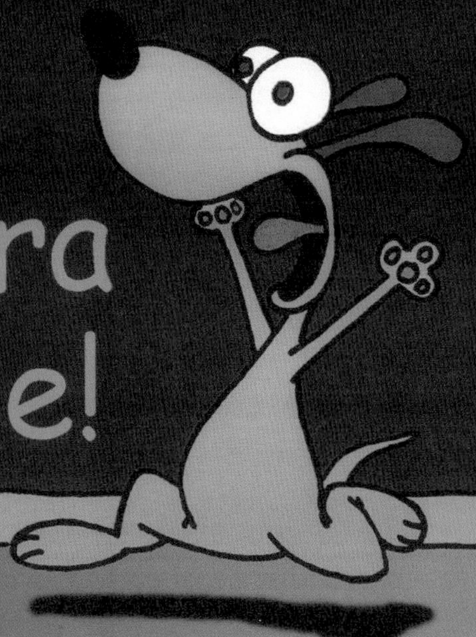

Is someone in the garage?

¿Hay alguien en el garaje?

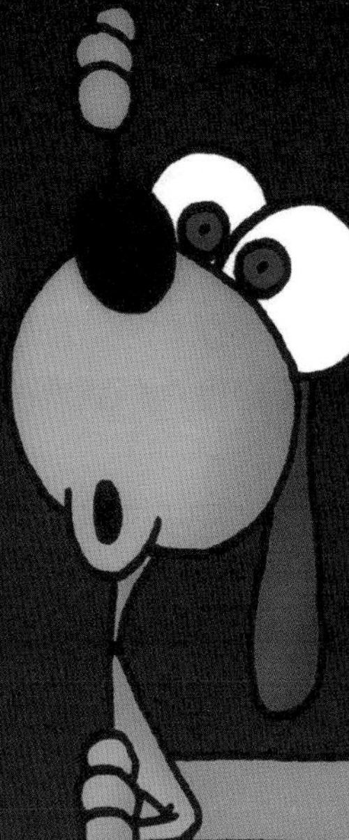

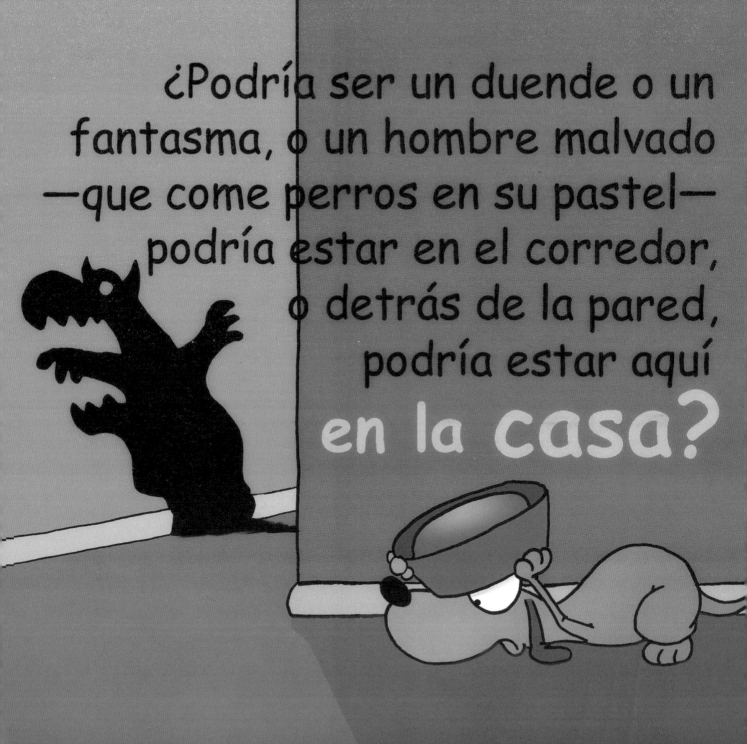

Could it be that a goblin or ghost, or a really bad guy —who eats dogs in his pie— may be down the hall, or behind the wall, could be here in our house?

O quizás sea un ratón.

Or, perhaps it's a mouse.

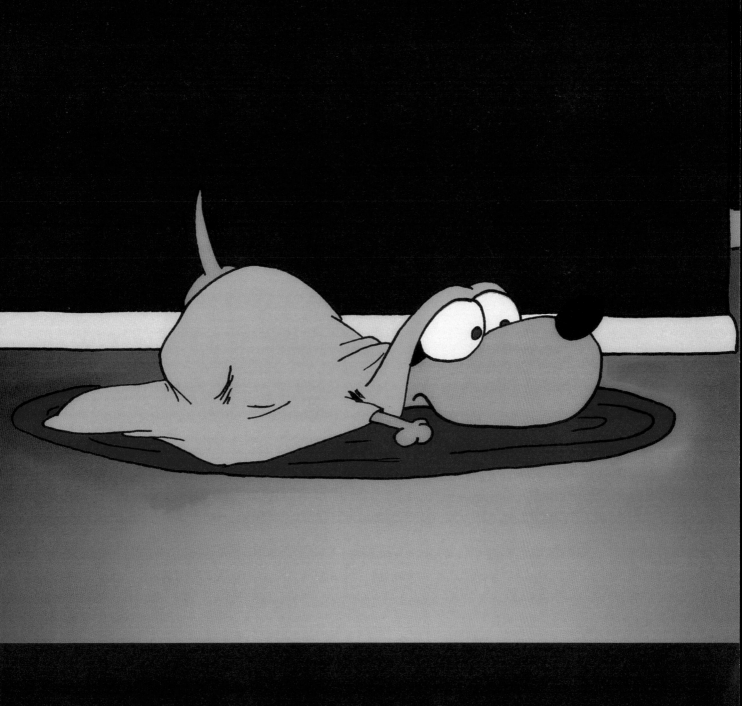

I think I know just what to do! I'll throw down the covers, and yell...

Yo creo saber exactamente qué hacer. Me echaré las frazadas encima y gritaré:

The End

Made in the USA
Charleston, SC
21 December 2011